S.F

CW00687368

THE MARINE PAINTINGS OF

Smitheman

S. Francis Smitheman

HALSTAR

First published in Great Britain in 2009

British Library Cataloguing-in-Publication Data
A CIP record for this title is available from the British Library

ISBN 978 1 906690 16 8

HALSTAR
Halsgrove House,
Ryelands Industrial Estate,
Bagley Road, Wellington, Somerset TA21 9PZ
Tel: 01823 653777   Fax: 01823 216796
email: sales@halsgrove.com

An imprint of Halstar Ltd, part of the halsgrove group of companies
Information on all Halsgrove titles is available at: www.halsgrove.com

Printed and bound by Grafiche Flaminia, Italy

CONTENTS

DEDICATION

To my wife whose idea this book was, and to my daughter Chantal and her husband Harris, who helped bring it to life,

ACKNOWLEDGEMENTS

To acknowledge all those who have contributed to the work in this book would require a book in itself. I would like, however, to thank most sincerely those who have commissioned work and often thereby led me into new subject areas. Also the galleries and institutions who have promoted my work, those who have bought paintings, those who have assisted me in my researches and given me so much technical help. I have mentioned some of these contributions in the text but I would like to acknowledge the following good people (in random order).

Alan Leesmith, Lyn Price, M. Henri Tournay and family. Lucia Harmston of Seaborne Interiors, Freddy Braun of Fartygsmagasnet, Hazel and Denis Smitheman, the Round Family, Mary and Trevor Wiltshire, Chantal Smitheman, Harris Padron, Robert Beresford, former Chairman Mott MacDonald Group. the Kobak family, Kathi and Chris Borchgrevink, the Doudoux family, Chris Arkel Peter Goodwin and Colin White of the Royal Naval Base and Museum, Jack Harker and family, Winefride Haynes, Margaret and Michael Rotchell, Charles Timberlake, Eileen and Howard Plocher, Henry Rogers and family, Doctors Mary and Kenneth McGee, Charles Mays Marine Artists.CO.UK, Captain T Frazer Morgan, former Captain HMS *Warrior*, Jane Skinner, Ken Jones of HMS *Warrior*, Whibley Galleries, Lisa Clayton Lady Cobham, Captain Simon Waite former Master *Cutty Sark*, The Vault- Brighton, Tony Bridgewater former Director the Trincomalee Project, Andre Debackere, Geof Lowels, Catherine Mason Pauntley Prints, Dr Hans Soop of the Royal Warship *Vasa*.
I would also like to acknowledge the courteous and helpful staff at Halstar. for their professional expertise.
Lastly, I want to say a special 'thank you' to Ema Exell, great photographer and computer wizard for all her help in pushing me into the electronic world.

Almost all my paintings are oil on canvas and measure either 36x24 in. (91x61 cm.) or 30x20 in. (76x51 cm.), a small percentage arc larger and the sketches or studies measure around 16x11 in. (41x28 cm.).

fsmitheman@btinternet.com

On his nomination as L'Artiste d'Honneur
in France the *Voix du Nord* stated
Like his illustrious predecessor Turner, Francis Smitheman
knows the sea and sailing perfectly and endeavours to
give his work authenticity. One finds all the world
of sea in his works, the ports, the craft, the human
activities on board, tempestuous seas and arctic wastes.

INTRODUCTION

FORMATION

I remember reading that General de Gaulle, former president of France, was privileged to have had a "Très bonne formation". My formation was not privileged but I cherish it all the same. It went something like this.

Blessed by being born into a poor family with caring parents, I spent from age five to fourteen in a Catholic school and with my two brothers sang in the Oratory choir each of us doing about five years. Thus, though ruffians by instinct, we were exposed to all the great masses from Bach to Beethoven. At a very young age one of my brothers took me to our local library to become a member. I immediately had access to the whole world of learning. I was, and still am, profoundly grateful for the library service. To me it has proved priceless.

To have some peace our parents packed us off on Sunday afternoons to Birmingham city centre where we invariably spent our time in its Museum and Art Gallery. By the time I left school I was familiar with most of the Art Gallery's permanent collections. Also I had found that I could draw and had had a painting of the liner *The Queen Mary* framed and hung on the classroom wall. Then in the face of discouragement I started to learn the violin.

WORK AND STUDY

At fourteen I started work in an aircraft factory working on the Hurricane and Lancaster. At sixteen I began to feel I had a vocation as a painter. At eighteen having endlessly built model aircraft during my boyhood and having the most romantic ideas about flying, I joined the RAF as a trainee Flight Engineer only to quickly lose the role, as the war's end being in sight, training numbers were cut. Becoming ground based held no romance for me and by then being politically conscious with socialist ideals I managed to transfer my national service to become a miner. There followed three very tough years that left me with the conviction that life, no matter how difficult it might become, would never be as bad. This has proved to be true. I did however manage to paint during these years, often pit-head scenes at sunrise conveying the joy of being at surface.

I managed to persuade my parents to partition a room so that I could have a studio. My Patron Saint was Van Gogh and I almost painted from the tube. Now I had a real hunger for education. Even whilst mining, following early shifts I managed to get to a 'crammer' school in Birmingham to study 'O' level subjects. These piecemeal studies went on for years until I reached University entrance level – all part time and paid for out of earnings. Needing work I obtained a job as a palette cleaner in a theatre scenery studio later progressing to scene painter and then assistant designer. I finally found a position at one of Rank's repertory theatres where we produced Shakespeare and Shaw plays as well as the more commercial popular works.

ART TRAINING

Some artists are strong enough to eschew a formal training. I am not one of them. I took some evening life classes. Then a generous friend obtained a grant of £60 from Rotary so that I could do a trial term on the four year National Diploma Design (Painting) or NDD course. I started on the two year course to Intermediate. At the end of the term the college decided to enter me for the

Intermediate examination and I passed it. I got a very small discretionary grant from the Trustees and by working evenings and weekends I went on two further years to the final NDD exam. I failed it, not I think through lack of work but rather the loss of five terms earlier on in the course meant that my work for the NDD was not mature enough.

During this period I had gained a small scholarship which enabled me to work in Paris for a period. The plan was that I should copy a work in the Louvre whilst studying the masters. There were many restrictions concerning; the size of the work, where it was situated in the gallery, the protection of the floor and so on. Finally I settled on Corot's "La Femme a la Perle" sometimes called the French Mona Lisa! I worked the hours allowed but the then would go out to study the Impressionists in the Jeux de Paume gallery and sketch in the 15eme Arrondissement before retiring to my pension where they always greeted me as "Monsieur Corot numéro deux"! The most lasting effect of the trip was my appreciation of the treatment of light and colour by Monet, Renoir and Bonnard to which I shall always aspire.

TRAVEL, A COMMISSION and MARRIAGE

Parallel to these events I had joined an interfaith group which worked for world change by changing individuals' moral standards. Noting a halt in my training they invited me to join an international force of some 300 people from a range of nations to take several didactic plays and musicals on a world tour. My theatre background made me a useful member of the team designing, mounting and travelling a heavily equipped tour. There followed nearly four years of travel and work in over thirty countries around the world. Now *that* was a privileged formation.

Eventually leaving the group I started out again as a sales assistant by day and a security guard by night to raise enough money to complete my art studies. Two years later I passed the NDD and then went on to take a Post Graduate course with the University of Birmingham ending with the Art Teacher's Diploma (ATD). These years were wonderful times. I learned so much. Art training then was based on a tradition which went back to the Renaissance – on the study of form, especially the human form and drawing was the premier skill. We painted from the human model three days a week. Composition took the other two days but we also took life classes in the evenings. No photographs, no computer manipulation. I reckon we were lucky.

An early commission after I had started teaching was a mural, about 30 feet by 10 feet for a new works canteen at Guest Keen and Nettlefolds in Birmingham which represented various departments of the factory. All the figures were life size and were portraits of well known characters.

During my Postgraduate year I had met my wonderful wife. She was already a grammar school teacher and we got married whilst I was a student and still rejoice that we did. The ATD course included crafts such as ceramics and metalwork. My tutors used to chide me by saying that all the objects I crafted were for my fiancée's bottom drawer.

Marrying my wife brought with it a new life. I obtained a post in one of the King Edward VI grammar schools and it was inspiring to work with such good colleagues. One of them had nurtured a fine madrigal group. On one occasion they were invited to sing at my "home" church, the Birmingham Oratory which had a rather splendid Baroque interior. The boys went to sing up in the choir stalls. It was reported to me later that they had counted "Smitheman" carved on the stalls eleven times. You can imagine how my credibility grew as a result.

HENRI and SAILING

As a young couple, then with a small child, we used to camp in the South of France. I used to go down early to the sea front near Cannes with my easel to paint attractive views (Boots the Chemists had offered to sell them in large stores where they had picture displays).

The owner of the camp at La Napoule saw me completing a work under the tent awning. We chatted and later we were invited up to his beautiful home. A wealthy man, Henri came from an historic family and possessed a collection of large family portraits dating back to the seventeenth century. He invited me to paint his companion and the work turned out well. This began a life long friendship and I have painted his children and recently their children.

My patron, Henri, was an experienced sailor once having owned a large schooner which sported a crew of sixteen and in which he had charted areas of the coast of Thailand. It was he, a few years later, who gave me my first marine commission: a large painting of a clipper, down at the bow, for his Salon. Happily this coincided with our ten year old daughter convincing me that to build a Mirror dinghy would be a splendid project for the both of us – and it was! We tried it out at Bosham and later took it on top of the car, with caravan in tow. to the Mediterranean. Next we chartered in England, then in France, finally buying a 22 ft Jeanneau "Captain" in France. The yacht had an inboard motor (which was unreliable) but in France, if you have a motor rated more than 9hp you have to have a certificate 'A' issued by the French Merchant Marine. This meant that you had to study the laws of sea practice and sit a written examination in French. You then had to take your boat, accompanied by an officer, out of port to the sea. You then did a circuit and returned to port all the while being tested for your competency – rather like a driving test. A force 7 was blowing when we did our individual tests and I was full of admiration for my wife for handling it. My wife had French Nationality so we bought the boat in her name so as to be able to keep it in France and avoid the exporting and importing obligatory for craft of foreign ownership. We both got our certificate 'A' but my wife was recorded as the boat's captain.

ART HISTORY

Professionally I had moved from the grammar school to a college of Higher Education concerned with training teachers to the B.Ed degree. I found myself lecturing increasingly on the History of Art. My own degree had been almost entirely practical so I took advice from Professor Miles at the Barber Institute in

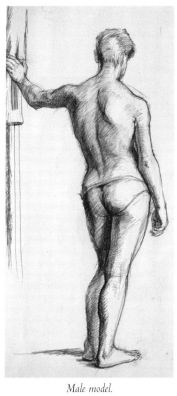

Male model.

Nude in studio.

Blonde female model.

Chantal's first oil painting.

Corot: La femme a la Perle (copy)

Paris café.

9

Birmingham and began a degree course with the Courtauld Institute of the University of London as an external student. Now a Head of Department at College I found these extra studies over a five year period hard going but also life changing in the way my knowledge and understanding was developed. Present day artists stand on the shoulders of all those who preceded them, inheritors of all their discoveries and stylistic developments, wealth indeed. Now my own life had been enriched by worldwide travel, sailing experience as a family and many insights into social history and the story of art. I had been painting a variety of subjects but without a progressive theme. It was a time for change.

WHY PAINT OLD SHIPS

I consider many old ships to be beautiful, like clippers or yachts. Or they can be intriguingly strange like the carracks and galleons with their high sterns built like castles. Often they are related to great events or exciting stories like HMS *Victory* and HMS *Bounty*. I had studied the Neo-classicists and Romantics such as Jacques Louis David, Ingres, Benjamin West and Turner. Their preoccupation with recreating the art of antiquity, or basing their work on subjects which drew on ancient morals for modern circumstances fascinated me.

Practically speaking, it means one chooses subjects which have some nobility in them, which can serve as uplifting role models. It seemed to me that marine painting would connect with all this. Since these subjects, in my case, are usually drawn from the past, I research them carefully. Here we are sometimes more fortunate than our forbears. To take HMS *Victory* at Trafalgar as an example, many artists depicted the battle in the early nineteenth century but their knowledge of the reality of the battle was often only sketchy. Today we have the advantage of two centuries of scholarship and museums full of documentation. For example at the Royal Naval Museum, I had access to a map which showed a marked course tracking every move *Victory* made in the 24hrs before she joined the battle. I was also able to read some of the British and French captains' log books, and in France I could learn how matters went from the French point of view. Also, of course, some of the ships have survived and been restored.

So I hope that some of the pictures in the book will lead readers to learn more about the extraordinary achievements of adventurous men in fine ships.

POLAR EXPLORERS, THE BEGINNING

My wife was now lecturing in Dress Design in a College of Higher education. The entrepreneur husband of one of her mature students visited us. He was enamoured of my work and described to me his great passion for the Antarctic. I had recently painted the *Pourquoi pas?* in her winter anchorage in Antarctica and on seeing it, he bought it immediately. Subsequently he asked me if he could commission me to paint the major explorers of Antarctica through history, to be purchased over a period of ten years. I agreed. Unfortunately his own fortunes waned and he was unable to buy the works that followed later. Nevertheless, I have gone on painting Antarctica and the Arctic for twenty years.

I had a long term Norwegian friend from my travelling days and he, as it were, picked up the baton and was instrumental in my painting the explorers Carsten E. Borchgrevink, Amundsen and Nansen. He, Chris Borchgrevink, organised a show of work in Norway, commissioned a number of works and, over the years, assisted my researches and always gave me positive support. Through him I was given access to the *Fram* which had been used by Nansen on a North Pole attempt and Amundsen the first to get to the South Pole. I did some of my painting on board the *Fram* with helpful criticism from the curator and the director of the National Maritime Museum, Oslo.

DUNKERQUE

My wife being French we visit family and friends in France for several weeks annually. After some years of progress as a marine artist, these contacts led to my being invited to a major exhibition in the Town Hall of Dunkerque as L'Artiste d'Honneur, the first time the award had been given to someone not French. I exhibited twenty eight works one of which was 'Dunkerque Harbour in 1909' which is described in the text.

Opened by the Senator Mayor, the occasion included a generous reception and almost overwhelmed us when the Mayor announced that the town would purchase the two most significant works in the show, one for the Musée des Beaux Arts, the other for a hospital. Later we also received a 7 ft x 5 ft poster of the Dunkerque painting which had been displayed around the town to greet the townsfolk for the New Year.

CUTTY SARK

Having nearly completed a painting of the *Cutty Sark*, I took it to the ship and met with the Captain, Simon Waite. He and his colleagues admired the painting, counselled me on several points and I was able to complete it. The painting was published as a print and it was decided to enhance it with two 'remarques' (small drawings on the lower border of the print drawn in pencil). The first would be a sail maker sitting on deck repairing a sail. The second would be sailors sheeting in one of the yards. This proved difficult so I returned to the *Cutty Sark* and asked the crew to pose for me. It was great fun with the Bosun directing and the men singing shanties while they hauled on the rope. The remarques were published, printed as if they were pencil drawings on the border of the colour print.

Prints of my *Cutty Sark* painting are sold on board ship and the Trust has frequently asked to use my images for various commemorations.

Another link with the *Cutty Sark* is that my sister in law, Barbara, is a Tudgay. F. Tudgay was a well known Victorian artist who painted the *Cutty Sark* in her heyday. The Cutty Sark Trust owns the painting and during an early restoration period, Tudgay's meticulous delineation was a reference which enabled them to rig the ship correctly. Some years ago I got permission to copy the painting so that Barbara's family could have a memento of her Grandfather's achievement.

Paris café drawing.

Mural 20 x 30 feet, for Guest Keen & Nettlefolds.

Painting stage scenery, Sri Lanka.

Sheeting in a yard on the Cutty Sark.

The artist on the Cutty Sark.

THE SS *GREAT BRITAIN*

I was invited by the S.S. *Great Britain* Project to paint the great ship arriving in New York in 1845. For me this was an honour and an exciting challenge. Regularly visiting the ship in Bristol, I got to know the people responsible for different aspects of the project and I realised that my research had to be as thorough as I could make it, including such details as the barrels on the quayside, at that time being hooped in wood not metal. Also the type of engine used to drive the nearby paddle tugs had to show the correct superstructures, since they were changed after 1845. My wife, a lecturer in Dress, helped me distinguish the costumes of American ladies from those of Europeans.

The ship herself is notable for her complex long hull form which goes from a sharp clipper-like entry back towards a marked outward bulge amidships. Also striking are the six masts, the foremost being vertical, whilst each following mast leans backwards each increasing further away from the vertical like a fan. After four months of work I finally delivered it to the Project for evaluation by the Committee. Prominent on that Committee was Sir Basil Greenhill, former director of the National Maritime Museum. He came out to tell me it was a fine 'pastiche' but wished to make a point about the rigging hawsers which ran down from the main mast forward to the bottom of the foremast. "These should advance a few millimetres" he said. So I had to take the work back home, four hours each way, to make this tiny change to the two cables. I later discovered that Sir Basil had published a paper on the ship which showed that the cables were anchored to a steel girder which supported the foremast and served to support the backward lean of the main mast and that this principle applied to all of the masts. Sir Basil had mathematically calculated the force and counterforce which Brunel had exploited in his design. No wonder he wanted the cables to hit the right point on the deck.

In spite of the comment 'pastiche' I was paid immediately, more than I had asked for, and was later asked to paint other works showing the ship's ever changing rig for the Project. One was only 24"x 18" and was offered in the annual raffle as a prize. It made £10,000 pounds for the restoration of one of the cabins.

LISA CLAYTON, LADY COBHAM

My brother and his wife who live near Birmingham told us they had met and got to know Lisa Clayton the 'Round the World Yachtswoman' and we learned of her incredible story. Dissatisfied with her rather aimless life and after only a limited experience as a yachtswoman, Lisa decided to sail single handed non-stop round the world.

Using all her savings she bought a rusty shell of a vessel and then with some support from Birmingham University and a great deal of hard work transformed it into a seaworthy yacht which she named *Spirit of Birmingham*. The story of her 31,000 mile journey and the wonderful but also terrifying experiences she encountered inspire awe and wonderment at her courage and determination.

We were inspired by what we heard and knowing that Lisa had returned to accolades, but also to serious debt, thought that perhaps I could paint the yacht in the wild Southern Ocean, and that we could produce a limited edition signed print which could make some money for her.

Although we and her team tried hard, the cost of advertising, painting, packaging and distribution was so high we could not afford the project. I had made three studies for the painting and Lisa had chosen one which I then carried out as a large oil painting on canvas.

Following her great adventure Lisa got a job as Managing Director of a catering company which organized functions at Hagley Hall the home of Viscount Cobham. In due course a romance flourished and Lisa Clayton became Lady Cobham. Some time later we received a letter from Lord Cobham asking if I still had the painting as he would like to buy it as a present for Lisa. This he wanted to be a surprise. So, one dark evening, we met him at the back of Hagley Hall and together quietly made our way to their apartment. Lord Cobham then called Lisa, who knew nothing of the arrangements, to come in to meet us and receive the painting. It was an occasion for many happy reminiscences and pink champagne.

SEABORN INTERIORS

My wife and I were looking at the craft in St Katherine's Dock, London, when we passed a shop with a long frontage displaying a wide range of maritime artifacts. These ran from diving helmets to ships lanterns, captains chairs to brass portholes; also visible were some fine marine paintings. We had with us some of my marine greeting cards. My wife insisted we go to see if the shop would sell them: we did. My expectation was resistance or polite refusal; instead we met the remarkable Lucia Harmston of Seaborne Interiors who was charming, warm and full of enthusiasm. We were invited to sit, chat and have coffee, she wanted to know about us and we felt an immediate rapport. Not only did she take the cards, she urged me to bring in my work, and thus began a friendship that continues to this day.

I brought in work and Lucia sold it. Most work was large and took a long time to create, therefore it was quite expensive but everything I took to Lucia she sold. She had a large international clientele and my work went out east to Japan and west to the USA. Furthermore, several of her customers gave me commissions.

PATRONS

One of Lucia's long standing clients was the American Charles Timberlake. He asked me if I would paint the great four mastered ship *Passat* which still exists and was moored at Travemunde in Germany.

Charles already owned my 'Flying Cloud' so, I thought this time I would paint an active harbour scene. *Passat* was built by Blom and Voss at Hamburg and frequently sailed from there. So we told him we would go to Hamburg to research the painting and he kindly arranged for us to meet a shipping business friend whilst we were there.

We booked a recommended hotel unknowing that two hotels in Hamburg bore the same name. Arriving at the airport we gave the hotel name to a taxi driver, explaining that we were researching the dock area. The hotel on arrival appeared rather modest but proved to be clean and efficiently run, though the night struck us as rather noisy with comings and goings.

The next day, when we met Charles' friends and told them where we were, the lady asked quietly whether we knew that we had spent the night in a brothel. However, all was well and being close to the great complex which is the port of Hamburg, together with some excellent books we found in town, I was well prepared to paint Charles' commission and I value it as one of my best works. I believe it hangs over his desk in the USA.

The owner of Seaborne Interiors, Freddy Braun, travels the world collecting maritime material and often tracks liners which, upon ending their lives, are stripped of their valuable interiors. At "Seaborne" you could find a complete panelled Captain's cabin, plus its furniture, to have built into your apartment on the Thames near Tower Bridge.

Freddy's base is Fartygsmagasinet in Stockholm and he befriended us on his visits to London. Gradually he became a significant patron commissioning large works such as the "Vasa", "Kronan" and "Gotheborg" and paintings relating to Amundsen, Nansen and Nordenskjold.

At the *Vasa* Museum in Stockholm Freddy introduced me to Dr Soop one of the ships restoration specialists who showed me how from microscopic particles from the stern they had been able to establish a great deal about the ships vivid colouring and gilding.

At the *Kronan* Museum we met Lars Einarsson who was chief diver at the wreck site. Whilst I was painting the *Kronan* he telephoned me to say that they had just raised a large section of the hull, and when I said I was working on it at that time, he promptly sent me transparencies of the section, so that I could authenticate my painting.

In the case of the *Gotheborg* when we visited the city we were told of the way the ship had capsized near her home port when she returned from a three year voyage to the East Indies. She had carried rattan, porcelain and tea in vast quantities. Our hosts gave us some small pieces of the original porcelain and a little of the tea which had been shipped in lead lined chests and had survived the wreck.

The *Gotheborg* has since been replicated to scale and with great fidelity to the original. She has made a repeat trip of the original ship, calling at Jakarta, Canton and Shanghai. Last year we saw her moored near the city looking quite sharp in her bright painting.

In the case of all of Freddy's paintings, he has organized the printing of large posters which sell at the ships' museums and contribute to their maintenance.

HMS *VICTORY*

One day, a lady appeared at my door asking if I was a marine painter – she was Mrs Mary Wiltshire. I replied in the affirmative so she came in and said she was looking for a painting for her husband's anniversary. We came to an agreement and I painted a work for her. The lady's husband Trevor Wiltshire was a Director of an electrical engineering company. His company was about to merge with another civil engineering company and both companies were to occupy some grand new building in Brighton. Later, I met Trevor who told me that he had suggested to the chairman of the soon to be merged company that I might contribute to the celebration by creating a painting.

Robert Beresford the company chairman visited me and having seen my work, commissioned me to paint a large work of the HMS *Victory* before the commencement of the Battle of Trafalgar. He was a man of stature with a dynamic personality and presented me with a series of bullets which the painting was meant to express to visiting clients. These included unity, determination, optimism and advancing forward with confidence.

It was a great experience painting the work which included visits from the chairman to give his opinions (though he always claimed that he had only called in for my wife's chocolate cake.) Eventually the painting was hung, beautifully lit, in a spacious entrance to Victory House.

During the painting process, I had several times visited HMS *Victory* at Portsmouth and did research at the Royal Naval Base Museum and Library. There I met Peter Goodwin, Keeper and Curator of HMS *Victory*. I learned that he was in the process of restoring the great ship, as far as scholarship could direct, to the appearance she had at Trafalgar. All this in readiness for the bicentenary celebrations in 2005. He generously helped me to get the details of my painting correct so as to reflect the most recent researches and work on the ship.

With the helpful collaboration of the Royal Naval Museum Trading Company we produced a print of the painting which was very successful and which lead me to paint more of Nelson's battles.

HMS *WARRIOR*

The *Warrior* lies within a few hundred yards of HMS *Victory* and I think that the staff there learned of the success of my *Victory* painting and print. This was at the time when *Warrior* was about to celebrate the tenth anniversary of the ship coming to Portsmouth.

Thus I was contacted by the Warrior Preservation Trust and asked if I would paint the great ship. It was a very positive experience since I was given any help I needed. We hit upon the idea of depicting *Warrior* leading ships of the channel squadron escorting the Royal Yacht Victoria and Albert in 1863. On board was her Royal Highness Princess Alexandra of Denmark, traveling to England to marry his Royal Highness the Prince of Wales, later to become King Edward VII.

It was a great help to be able to frequently visit the actual ship and I completed it in about ten weeks. It was well received and it was decided to produce a limited edition print. There was soon to be a major ceremony to celebrate the anniversary and the ship's patron Princess Alexandra was to attend. It was a joyous occasion. The ship was dressed overall and a Marine brass band played to all the many people who had worked on and generously supported the ship. Descending sun bathed the *Warrior* in a golden light and the Princess wandered the crowded deck. It seemed to us that she spoke to everyone within reach. Later in the Captain's cabin the Princess

Lisa Clayton back home.

Gladys and Francis Smitheman.

Princess Alexandra in the Captain's cabin, studying the painting of HMS Warrior.

Prince Phillip questioning me about the painting.

was presented with NoI of 500 limited edition prints of the painting. She compared it with the original work and chatted amiably with my wife, promising to find a special place for the picture. Some months later Prince Phillip visited HMS *Warrior* and I was invited to meet him and show him the painting. The work now has a permanent place on board.

There is a fun sequel to this commission. Apparently on October 21st all the Royal Naval ships commemorate the Victory of Trafalgar, often with a dinner on board. HMS *Warrior* follows this tradition and we were invited. It was an august occasion with the Lieutenant General representing the Queen, and many other distinguished guests including a visiting American Admiral who had left a Battle Fleet moored out in the Channel.

Captain Bawtree welcomed his guests and maintaining another Royal Navy tradition raised a toast to Admiral Nelson before he toasted Her Majesty the Queen (I believe this is the only occasion in the Services that this happens). Coming to the end of his speech, he said, rather guardedly, that he had to advise the company that we had "the enemy in our midst". He then indicated my wife who is French. "However", he countered, "since we have been drinking good French wine" (bottled with a large Warrior label on it) "I think we can make an exception".

THE SAGA OF THE PAINTING "THE BATTLE OF THE NILE"

As part of a series of Nelsonian works I painted the Battle of the Nile; an absorbing subject in terms of battle strategy and for its significance in European history. I did considerable research including a model map to see how the vessels were positioned.

When nearly complete I went to the Royal Naval Base at Portsmouth to consult with Colin White the Nelson scholar. I think he found the painting impressive but had one major misgiving. Colin White said that no one knew with precision what the position of Nelson's *Vanguard* was at this point in the battle, but he had a 'hunch' that Nelson would have been much closer to the French line. Very disappointed I went home realizing that the change suggested would involve a ruinous repaint and so decided that I would create a second painting.

The second painting met with Colin's approval and after launching it as a print which sold at the R.N. Museum Victory Shop, I sent it to Christie's. The work was accepted and I was later pleased to learn that it had been sent with other work to Christie's in Paris as a promotion for the London sale.

A week before the sale date, I heard from the head of Maritime Sales that on its return, my painting had been damaged and that there was an eight inch tear in the middle of the canvas. I was told that Christie's had an excellent restorer who could repair the damage and that they would like to continue to include it in the sale.

I agreed to the repair providing that I inspect the work before the sale and that no buyer should be ignorant of the damage. When I saw the repaired work I was astonished. I could see no evidence on the face of the canvas though the back wore a large patch. Apparently there was considerable interest from the public, and the painting sold well above the highest estimate.

THE ROYAL MINT

The Royal Mint is known, of course, for producing millions of coins. But it has also produced much jewelry and many objets d'art.

In 2004, staff from the Royal Mint visited the Royal Naval Base looking for items they could offer to support the celebrations forecast for 2005. They saw my print, of HMS *Victory*, liked it and contacted me. The first outcome was a joint operation to produce a new large classic print in a limited edition of 1805 copies. This was a new departure for the Royal Mint. Happily, the whole edition sold out very quickly.

The next development was that the Royal Mint decided to commission me to paint a new version of the Battle of Trafalgar for early 2005 – a splendid challenge! By the time I had completed the work, it was decided to auction it on the internet. In preparation for the event, I was asked to record a brief televised presentation of the painting and of Nelson's strategy. Remarkably the painting reached £21,000 in auction.

The Royal Mint went on to produce thirteen more limited edition prints of my work and commissioned three more paintings. It was most interesting to work for such an institution, to experience its efficiency and to meet its exacting standards

POSTSCRIPT

It seems extraordinary to me that after a long life working I still want to paint more than I have time for, and still experience the same sense of hope and excitement I had as a young student. It is a precious gift and I shall always be grateful to those who have nurtured and contributed to it.

HISTORIC SHIPS

Previous page:
**THE BATTLE OF
THE *MARY ROSE* 1548**

MARY ROSE 1545,
A PORTRAIT

The *Mary Rose* was built in 1510. Here she is shown after a rebuild in 1545 and now flagship of Henry VIII's navy. The king witnessed her leading an attack on a large French force off the Isle of Wight when she heeled and sank.

The ship was rediscovered and excavated during the period 1965 to 1982. Most of one side of the vessel was salvaged together with many remarkable artefacts.

The painting was researched at the museum and it was intended to be reproduced as a poster to attract public support for the ship's restoration.

THE BATTLE OF THE *MARY ROSE*
THE ENGLISH FLEET WITH THE *MARY ROSE* RESISTING THE FRENCH OFF PORTSMOUTH JULY 19th, 1548

In 1544, the English captured Boulogne. In retaliation, the French decided to try to destroy the English Fleet at Portsmouth. D'Annebault, the French Admiral, ordered his oared galleys to advance upon the English ships to draw them away from the protective land forts.

Taking advantage of a rising wind, the *Mary Rose* (right) advanced on the galleys, then whilst going about, suddenly heeled over. Her lower gun ports being open, water poured into the hull. This, together with the weight of the guns and personnel high on the ship, caused her to capsize and the vessel sank with a loss of nearly 700 souls.

The battle continued and eventually the French were obliged to withdraw to France and blockade Boulogne.

In recent times a large part of the hull of the *Mary Rose* has been raised from the sea bed and is on show in a Museum in Portsmouth's dockyard.

Below: **AN ALTERNATIVE DESIGN FOR THE *MARY ROSE* BATTLE**

THE *VASA*, SUNDAY AUGUST 10th 1628

The *Vasa* was a magnificent spectacle as she set forth on her maiden voyage from Stockholm. At first there was a gentle breeze filling her sails but then a great gust of wind suddenly caused the ship to heel and she took water through her open gun ports. Gradually the hull flooded and she went right over on her side and sank after a voyage of only 1,300 metres, "under full sail pennants and all" and with the loss of some 50 persons.

Three centuries later in 1961, great efforts were made to salvage the ship, which having been remarkably protected by the lower salt content of the Baltic waters, was able to be towed, floating, to safety.

The *Vasa* is now preserved in a purpose-built museum in Stockholm providing us with an absorbing study of early shipbuilding and illuminating the lives of the seamen who manned her.

**THE SWEDISH SHIP *KRONAN* FIGHTING THE DANES AND
THE DUTCH AT THE BATTLE OF OLUND JULY 1676**

In her day, the *Kronan* was the most powerful warship afloat. In an early action, against the combined Dutch and Danish fleet, *Kronan* fought well and sailing astern of the Dutch Admiral's flagship she loosed a broadside which tore such a gaping hole in the Dutchman's stern that, according to a Swedish gunner, you could drive a coach and four horses through it.

A week later, however, the fleet met again and whilst under full sail in a gusting wind, *Kronan* made a sharp turn and the great ship simply capsized. As her mast reached the water, a violent explosion from the magazine ripped her apart. She sank with the loss of some 800 men. A contemporary account describes how one Anders Sparrfelt was blown sky high by the explosion. He flew over two enemy ships before landing safely in the sail of a Swedish vessel.

He survived to reach high office in the Swedish Navy.

KRONAN DETAIL AND DRAWING

The detail shows the stern of the Dutch Admiral's flagship.
The drawing shows an alternative design.

HMS *BOUNTY* AT MATAVAI BAY, TAHITI, 1788

HMS *Bounty* was commissioned to collect breadfruits from Tahiti and take them to the British West Indies where they were to be cultivated for consumption. She departed in April 1787 commanded by Captain William Bligh and after a hazardous voyage of 27,000 miles anchored at Matavai Bay, Tahiti in October 1788.

In the painting she is seen in calm waters inside the reef in sight of Point Venus named by Captain Cook after his observatory was set up to watch the transit of Venus. After six months of an idyllic life, *Bounty* set out for the West Indies. Three weeks later, led by Fletcher Christian, many of the crew rebelled and Captain Bligh and 18 members of the crew were set adrift in an open boat. They sailed a distance of almost 4,000 miles before reaching Timor and safety.

The mutineers wandered the Pacific seeking refuge and ended on Pitcairn Island (where some of their descendents still live) so as to avoid discovery by passing ships. Eventually, *Bounty* was burned lying off Pitcairn.

MODEL OF HMS *BOUNTY* BUILT BY THE ARTIST AND FULLY RIGGED BY HIS WIFE AND DAUGHTER

25

HMS _WARRIOR_ ESCORTING THE ROYAL YACHT _VICTORIA & ALBERT_, MARCH 1863

The vessels are seen crossing the English Channel leading ships of the Channel squadron. On board the Royal Yacht was HRH Princess Alexandra of Denmark travelling to England to marry HRH the Prince of Wales, later to be King Edward VII.

The _Warrior_ was built in response to the French who had built the _Gloire_, the first ironclad. The British built a much bigger ship both iron hulled and iron clad, thus at the time she became the most formidable battleship the world had ever known. Fortunately, she never had to fire a shot in anger. Fully restored, _Warrior_ now lies at Portsmouth dockyard where she can be visited.

The detail shows the Royal Yacht _Victoria and Albert_.

MARIQUITA, OCTAVIA AND NORADA RACING IN THE SOLENT AUGUST 7th 1911

Mariquita is shown racing ahead of *Octavia* and *Norada* in the 19 metre class race at Cowes Regatta. Such yachts up to 25 metres long and weighing 100 tonnes were called "greyhounds". Although they strike us as enormous now, their size was considered quite reasonable at that time.

THE *GEORG STAGE II*, DENMARK

By law, every young Dane who wishes to go to sea and serve on deck must receive three months training at a college or aboard a cadet ship. The full rigged *Georg Stage*, built in 1935 serves this role admirably, sailing in the Baltic and the North Sea. Remarkably, over 8,000 boys have been thus trained on the *Georg Stage II* or her predecessor *Georg Stage I*.

THE *THERMOPYLAE* PICKING UP A PILOT OFF DUNGENESS 1868

This painting is based on the log of the *Thermopylae* which describes arriving at late afternoon and taking on board a Pilot to take her round to the Thames. The Pilot boat has dropped the Pilot in a small boat which he then rows to the Jacob's ladder of the ship. Once aboard, his boat would be left to drift whilst the Pilot boat would tack round to collect it, often single-handed!

Thermopylae was probably the fastest and best all-round clipper ever built. She was composite built – wood planking over an iron frame – by Walter Hood of Aberdeen for the White Star Line. She could load 1000 tons of tea though she spent most of her career in the Australian wool trade. On her maiden voyage, she broke the record on each leg being only 60 days from Pilot to Pilot London – Melbourne, 28 days Pilot to Pilot Newcastle – Shanghai and then 91 days from Foochow to London.

SIR JAMES CLARKE ROSS DISCOVERING THE MOUNTAIN WHICH HE NAMED AFTER HIS SHIP *EREBUS*, JANUARY 1841

The first ships to penetrate the pack ice of Antarctica were *Erebus* and *Terror* under Sir James Clarke Ross. Sent by the Royal Navy to explore the southern latitudes and search for the magnetic pole, he discovered Victoria Land and entered the sea that now bears his name. He also discovered Ross Island, Mt Erebus and the great cliffs of the Ross Ice Shelf. He returned to Hobart but sailed south again the following summer and traced the ice shelf further east reaching 78 degrees south; a record that stood until 1900.

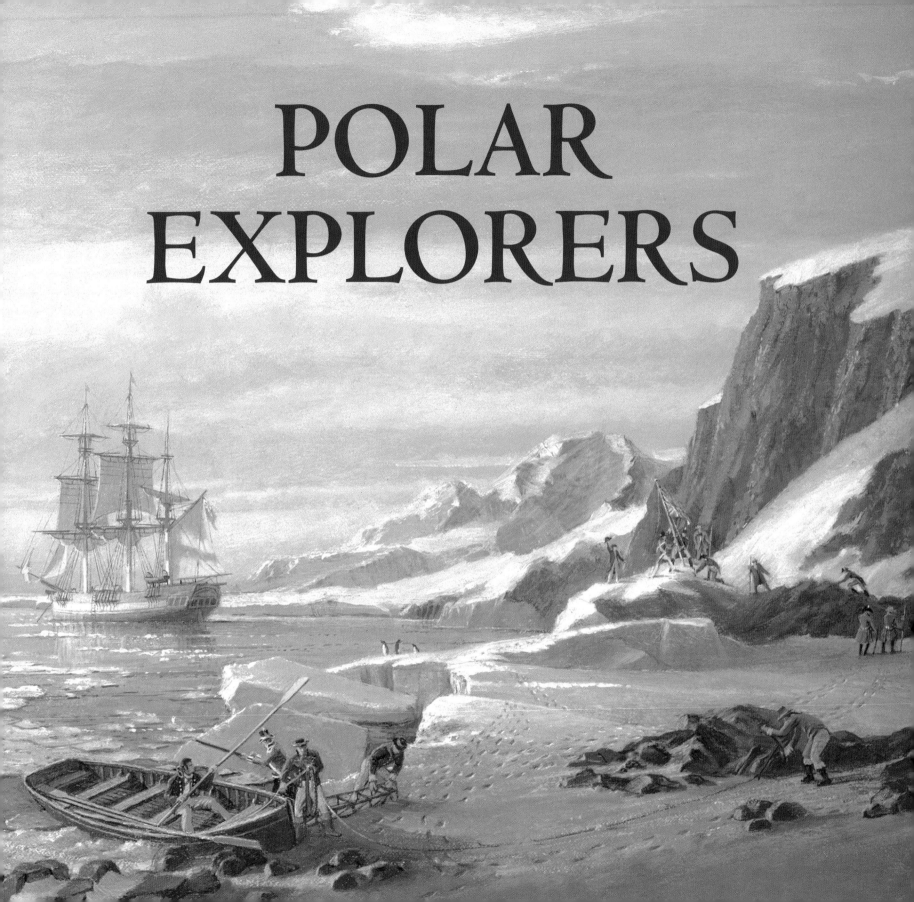

POLAR EXPLORERS

ASTROLABE & *ZELEE* IN THE WEDDELL SEA

"We then had to use every means at our disposal. Men climbed down onto the ice to tie ropes to the floes… those who remained on board hauled on them to move painfully forward, while others tried to push the ice aside with pincers and pickaxes in order to regain the open sea." Dumont d'Urville describing the problems faced by the two ships in the Weddell Sea.

The Frenchman, following the tracks of James Weddell, was trying to get as close as possible to the South Pole.

N.A.E. NORDENSKIOLD'S EXPEDITION THROUGH THE NORTHEAST PASSAGE 1878-1879

Nordenskiold, effectively a Swedish explorer, discovered the Northeast Passage on an epic voyage in the ship *Vega*. The Northeast Passage is the maritime route of the Arctic ocean north of Siberia leading from the Atlantic to the Pacific via the Bering Strait.

Right:
NORDENSKIOLD STUDYING THE ROUTE

RESOLUTION AND _ADVENTURE_ NEAR ANTARCTICA 1773

Captain James Cook circumnavigated Antarctica in two small ships, _Resolution_ and _Adventure_ travelling more than 60,000 miles (97,000 Km). The aim was to see if there was an uninhabited habitable land mass south of the known world.

We see the ships early in 1773 when, near what is now called Enderby Land, they edged along the ice, probing for a gap which would take them further south, sometimes using a ship's boat to explore a channel to find clear water beyond. One can imagine every sound echoing in the vast stillness and how remote and insignificant each man must at times have felt. Cook came to believe that no such land existed unless it were at the Pole itself.

NANSEN WITH *FRAM* IN RAFTING ICE

"Behind Amundsen, Shackleton, Scott and Perry looms the spirit of Fridjof Nansen (1861 – 1930), the father of modern polar exploration."
Roland Huntford

THE VOYAGE OF THE *FRAM* 1893-1896

Two questions preoccupied many northern explorers in the last quarter of the nineteenth century.

Was there an open sea passage over Russia between Greenland and the North of Asia and the Bering Sea? Did the Arctic current flow from east to west and if it did so, did it move northerly and thereby reach nearer the Pole?

With respect to the both questions, Nansen believed that the answer was "yes". He had constructed a specially designed craft that was capable of being frozen into the ice and survive thus without damage by virtue of its rounded bottom which would be squeezed upwards by pressure ice rather than be crushed.

So Nansen and twelve men entrusted their fates to the ice, winds and sea. They sailed in the *Fram* over the north of Norway and on to Siberia, then north into the ice pack in the hope that they would drift with the ice currents back in a north-easterly direction towards their goal. Two of them would then leave *Fram* to try to reach the Pole.

The painting illustrates a dramatic event at the New Year of 1895 when the *Fram*, gripped in ice, was overtaken by rafting ice which gradually bore down and threatened to engulf the craft. Serious preparations were made to abandon ship. Nansen wrote "We are like tiny dwarfs in a struggle with Titans; one must save oneself with cunning and ingenuity if one is to escape from this giant fish which rarely lets go what it has once seized."

NANSEN LEAVING FOR THE POLE MARCH 14th 1895

Fridtjof Nansen, with his vessel the *Fram*. made an attempt to get to the North Pole His plan was to sail east along the North East Passage into the ice cap and then drift with the north-westerly ice flow which would bring him nearer the Pole. Then, with a colleague, three kayaks and dogs they would leave the ship and travel due north to their goal. The painting shows Nansen leading the team in the light of torches placed out by his crew to bid him a good start.

The expedition failed but created heroes of Nansen and his companion Johansen for their courage in surviving a terrible journey back.

THE *BELGICA* NEAR ANVERS ISLAND, GRAHAM LAND, JANUARY 1898

The Belgian converted whaler *Belgica* is seen moored near Anvers Island. The *Belgica* was the first ship to penetrate this part of the Antarctic Peninsula and this strait, much used by whalers after its discovery, was named after Adrian de Gerlache, the *Belgica's* Captain.

Freshwater on the *Belgica* was supplied by a snow melter – a converted condenser from the engine room – and so we see on the right a crew member gathering frozen snow. The same contraption could be adapted to burn seal blubber as fuel so other crew are seen hauling a dead seal towards the ship's boat for transport to the *Belgica*.

Unhappily, due to delayed progress, *Belgica* hit pack ice and became imprisoned. There followed a 13 month nightmare; two months of unbroken darkness, more than a year of snow and hail, deafening winds, illness, insanity and for one of the explorers, Danco, death. On March 14th 1899, the expedition finally emerged from the ice and began the long journey home.

THE *SOUTHERN CROSS* IN ANTARCTICA WITH CARSTEN E. BORCHGREVINK

This expedition, led by the Norwegian C. E. Borchgrevink, was financed by the British and became the first party to set foot on the Antarctic mainland in 1899. They made a significant contribution to the discovery of Antarctica and valuable naturalist material was brought back to the British Museum for research. The *Southern Cross* is seen at Cape Adair. Borchgrevink, (standing) and Hansen are recovering a dead seal. One of the Lap crew is bringing stores from the expedition's hut seen in the distance. The hut still exists to this day.

The sketch left shows the *Southern Cross* leaving Tower Bridge at the commencement of her voyage south.

The painting was commissioned by Christopher Borchgrevink, a friend of the artist, who is distantly related to the explorer. In Norway, the Borchgrevink clan is quite a big one and when the painting was exhibited at a large gathering in northern Norway, several other Borchgrevinks wanted to commission another version of the subject.

THE *SOUTHERN CROSS* AT CAPE ADAIR 1899 VERSION 2

When the first painting was exhibited in Norway several other Borchgrevinks wanted to commission further versions.

Below:
CAPTAIN C.A. LARSEN'S *JASON* IN THE LEMAIRE CHANNEL c.1893

The Norwegian Captain Larsen, in his vessel the *Jason* combined whaling reconnaissance and sealing, as shown here, with the careful exploration of Graham Land. During the 1890s such whalers were instrumental in stimulating scientific interest in Antarctica on an international scale.

THE *FRANCAIS* IN ANTARCTICA

Dr Jean Charcot inherited a fortune from his father, gave up medicine and pursued his true vocation as an explorer. He invested in the building of the *Francais*, specially designed for Antarctic exploration. In 1904 he sailed to the Antarctic Peninsula and wintered at Booth Island. Over two summers, he charted islands and extended the survey of the western side of the peninsula.

THE *POURQUOI PAS?* FROZEN IN HER WINTER ANCHORAGE, PETERMAN ISLAND 1909

In his first ship, the *Francais*, Francois Charcot 'Polar gentleman, explorer, scientist, doctor, philosopher' accurately surveyed the western side of the Antarctic Peninsula during 1903-05. Charcot then had built the most modern polar ship known, the *Pourquoi pas?* In 1908-10 he extended his work along the peninsula, exploring 1,240 miles (2,000 km) of unknown coastline.

Charcot carried with him a distinguished team of scientists and created the best conditions he could for their work. This included a gramophone on which, especially on Sundays, he played concerts of popular music. It is said that these fascinated the penguins which came in numbers to listen.

AMUNDSEN RETURNS TO THE *FRAM*
AND GREETS THE CAPTAIN

The *Fram* had brought Amundsen, his colleagues and stores to the Bay of Whales in January 1911. It then sailed to Buenos Aires whilst the party made their preparations during the Antarctic winter, in readiness for an attempt on the Pole.

The attempt was made on September 8th and they reached the Pole on December 14th 1911. Returning without mishap, they reached "Framheim" their base at the Bay of Whales. Extraordinarily, *Fram* returned the very next day after its long absence.

The painting shows the five men who had reached the pole being the first to greet the Captain. The five who had manned Framheim, the base camp, follow to join the joyful reunion.

THE POLAR VICTORS RACE BACK TO THE *FRAM*

On December 14th 1911, Amundsen with four companions and eighteen dogs planted the Norwegian flag at the South Pole after a journey of 57 days. Amundsen left a letter for Scott and the group returned to their base at the Bay of Whales.

We see the dogs leading Amundsen and his colleagues racing down from their base "Framheim" above the cliffs followed by those who had manned the base during the attempt on the Pole.

The painting was commissioned by the distinguished Norwegian Christopher Borchgrevink.

THE *TERRA NOVA* AT CAPE EVANS IN SIGHT OF MT EREBUS WITH SCOTT AND WILSON PREPARING THEIR ATTEMPT ON THE POLE

The *Terra Nova*, a 700 tonne coal-burning whaler built in 1884, arrived at Cape Evans, Antarctica in early January 1911. Once arrived activity onshore was furious. The weather was fine and morale high. By the end of the day, the hut site had been leveled and the relieved animals and many supplies had been landed. By the 17th January, the hut was complete. Scott wrote: "We find we have a splendid collection of gramophone records."

During the winter of 1911 the hut became not only the expedition's living quarters but, under Scott's influence, like the wardroom of a Royal Naval vessel. Edwardian values were cherished and it became, as it were, an outpost of the Empire.

As well as the base for the attempt on the Pole, the hut was the departure point for two other expeditions, an eastern party to explore King Edward VII Land, and a western party to investigate the glacier region to the west of Mc Murdo Sound. Both of these proved to be extremely hazardous and arduous. Cherry Garrared wrote "Such extremity of suffering cannot be measured. Madness or death may give relief...we on this journey were already beginning to think of death as a friend." It was thus that Mt Erebus, once sited, became a 'welcoming beacon' and the hut a longed for haven of safety and comfort. Sadly, at the end, they did not play this role for Scott and his valiant friends.

SCOTT, EXHAUSTED AT THE POLE

GRITVIKEN WHALING STATION, SOUTH GEORGIA

Gritviken, for forty years was the capital of the Norwegian whaling industry. It was also very close to where Shackleton arrived after his epic journey to find safety and help rescue his colleagues from the lost *Endurance* marooned on Elephant Island.

The sketch was made in preparation for a larger work in my series on Antarctica. I was told that to show whales being flayed was now considered objectionable. This struck me as unreasonable since the painting related to an historical reality when whales provided practical materials for millions of humans including oil which illuminated their homes.

SHACKLETON'S *ENDURANCE* BESET BY ICE IN THE WEDDEL SEA

Shackleton's epic Antarctic expedition was beset by problems including the loss of his ship the *Endurance*. It was only by extreme determination and great self sacrifice that he was able to save his colleagues from death. Here the *Endurance* is gripped by pressure ice which will eventually crush and sink it. For safety, the dogs have been taken off and housed in "dogloos". Shackleton is making a nightly round to make sure that all is well.

LONDON'S RIVER

THE UPPER AND LOWER POOLS OF THE THAMES

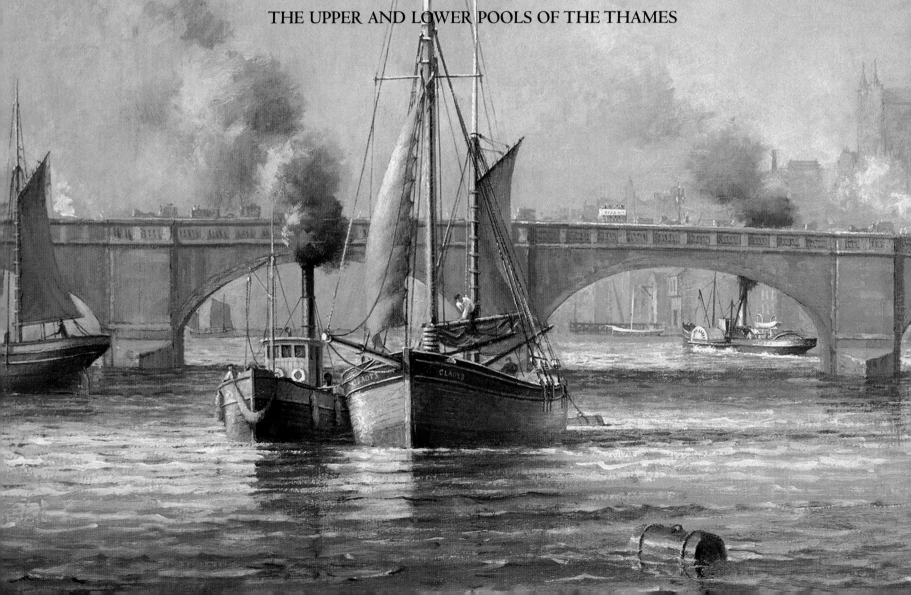

THE LOWER POOL OF THE THAMES CIRCA 1904

A wooden barque, having made an occasional visit to the Upper Pool, is being towed down river by two tugs having passed through Tower Bridge. To the left is the *Regina Elena*, a steel barque from Italy which was later to form part of the famous P-Line and sail in the Chilean nitrate trade. Later rechristened *Ponape*, she was still seen on the Thames as late as 1936. The paddle steamer seen on the right is probably the *Swallow*.

THE *CUTTY SARK* BEING TOWED UP TO TOWER BRIDGE 1895

The *Cutty Sark* is seen being towed up to Tower Bridge which had recently been opened in 1894.

The ship is rigged pretty much as she was in her glory days. Designed to be very fast in order to win that premium paid to the ship bringing home the first tea of the season, she frequently competed with other ships. After joining the wool trade, from Australia, she took part in the wool race in 1885 and was undisputed winner making Sydney to London in 73 days.

After many years, when the *Cutty Sark* was 53 years old she was bought by the British Captain Wilfred Downman, he restored her and used her as a training ship. Finally in 1952 the *Cutty Sark* Preservation Society was formed and she was taken to the specially built dry dock in Greenwich.

The first Captain George Moodie, said that she was "a grand ship, and a ship that will last forever." In spite of her recent misfortune by fire, one has no doubt that she will rise again 'Phoenix-like' as a monument to the great age of sail.

A SQUARE RIGGER BEING EASED BY A TUG INTO A MOORING NEAR THE OLD LONDON BRIDGE AROUND 1900

THE *CUTTY SARK* TOWING PAST GREENWICH

The *Cutty Sark* is being towed down river, assisted on her starboard side by a second tug, passing her future resting place – Greenwich.

The nearby hay barge employs the same breeze as the clipper to sail up to the city with its cargo to feed the capital's thousands of horses. In the distance we see Greenwich Hospital, built as a home for retired seamen, and described as the grandest almshouse in the world.

SKETCH OF THE *SOUTHERN CROSS*
ABOUT TO LEAVE FOR ANTARCTICA

THAMES BARGES AND AN
AUXILIARY UNDER TOW

THE *BURY ST EDMUNDS* BEING TOWED UP TO TOWER BRIDGE

Tower Bridge has been opened to allow the barque *Bury St Edmunds* to proceed into the upper pool. Another square sail rigged vessel is moored to the left of the bridge. Both craft are exploiting the calm conditions to dry their sails. A paddle steamer full of trippers is making downstream for Greenwich. The lighters (barges) in midstream are swinging on a slack tide whilst one of the lightermen is preparing to receive a workmate who is sculling a small boat towards him. In due course they will ferry one of the lighters using long oars or sweeps.

THE WINDJAMMER *PASSAT* NEAR TOWER BRIDGE
CIRCA 1930

The subject of the painting is, in one sense the last days of sail, in another, it is the luminosity that can pervade a river scene at evening.

The *Passat* was one of a series of P-sailing ships all built by Blom and Voss at Hamburg between 1916 and 1920. These large, mostly four-masted barques were designed to sail with small crews carrying nitrate from Chile and grain from Australia to Europe. Their success in competing with steam vessels was, however, short lived. Several vessels were lost and others became sail training ships. Fortunately *Passat* survived the war and is still afloat at Travemunde, Germany and used as a summer camp for the young.

63

SAIL AND STEAM, EVENING

The nineteenth century saw steam gradually overtake sail as the means of driving vessels. This painting tries to evoke the 'sunset' of commercial sailing ships by juxtaposing a tall three-masted barque moored with a passenger liner moving down river.

This was painted for a marvellous lady "Lucia", who managed Seaborne Interiors on St Katherine's Dock (just visible on the painting). There you could buy anything from a cleat to a ship's binnacle to the whole cabin of a well known, now 'retired', liner. You could also buy some good marine paintings by reputable artists. Lucia managed to sell my works worldwide including Europe, Japan and the Americas. (The store's owner Freddy Braun gets mention on my *Vasa* page.)

THE 'NIGHT WATCHMAN', DOWNSTREAM OF THE LOWER POOL

It would seem that in either the vessel or the warehouse there is some cargo of value since a night watchman has been employed to look after things. He is well organized with a hut, brazier, some wood, a chopper and block. He even has a mate. This sort of frontage is reminiscent of Conrad's "mad jumble of begrimed walls" and we are not far from Jacob's Island where Dickens sited the final chase of Bill Sykes in *Oliver Twist*. Such small buildings were swept away in the redevelopment of the 1890s and replaced with multistoried warehouses and mobile cranes. These in turn have become redundant and some have now been converted into luxury apartments.

DISCOVERY TOWING UP TO LONDON BRIDGE

Discovery was built in 1901 for the Antarctic expedition of the British Royal Geographical Society. She was given a massively reinforced hull for survival in ice and a screw and rudder that could be hoisted into vertical shafts to avoid ice damage. Her interior was fully fitted out with laboratories including a magnetic laboratory. We tend to call her Scott's *Discovery* because as commander, Robert Scott led an expedition in *Discovery* from New Zealand in 1901 returning to England in 1904 after spending a summer frozen in the ice. The expedition returned to adulation and respect – men who had prevailed in the icy fastnesses became heroes! This concept was reinforced by Scott's tragic journey to the South Pole when he and four of his colleagues were frozen to death on the return journey (the vessel then used was the *Terra Nova*). After a varied career including Canadian and French ownership, *Discovery* made another Antarctic voyage in 1931 under the leadership of Sir Douglas Mawson. She was then taken by the British Boy Scouts as a training ship moored on the Thames in the centre of London. Eventually she was repatriated to Dundee, where she had been built, and lies in a permanent berth as a Museum Ship.

The painting depicts how she would have looked towing up to her station on the Thames.

THE *CUTTY SARK* IN THE LOWER POOL c.1895

The *Cutty Sark* is being towed down river from the recently opened Tower Bridge. I think I took some liberty with showing so many sails set, though ships did try to dry out wet sails when they could. I worked closely with the Master and crew when painting the work and they seemed to see nothing untoward.

HMY *BRITANNIA* LEAVING TOWER BRIDGE FOR THE LAST TIME

Her Majesty's Yacht *Britannia* was decommissioned on December 11th 1997 at Portsmouth having been in the service of Her Majesty for nearly 44 years. After being 'paid off' she made a tour ending with a farewell from Tower Bridge on November 21st when she flew her paying off pennant. The pennant is usually the length of the ship plus one foot for every year that the vessel has been in commission – 456 feet in the case of *Britannia*.

A member of the crew told me that flying it was a challenge since it could behave wildly and even get caught in the ship's screws.

71

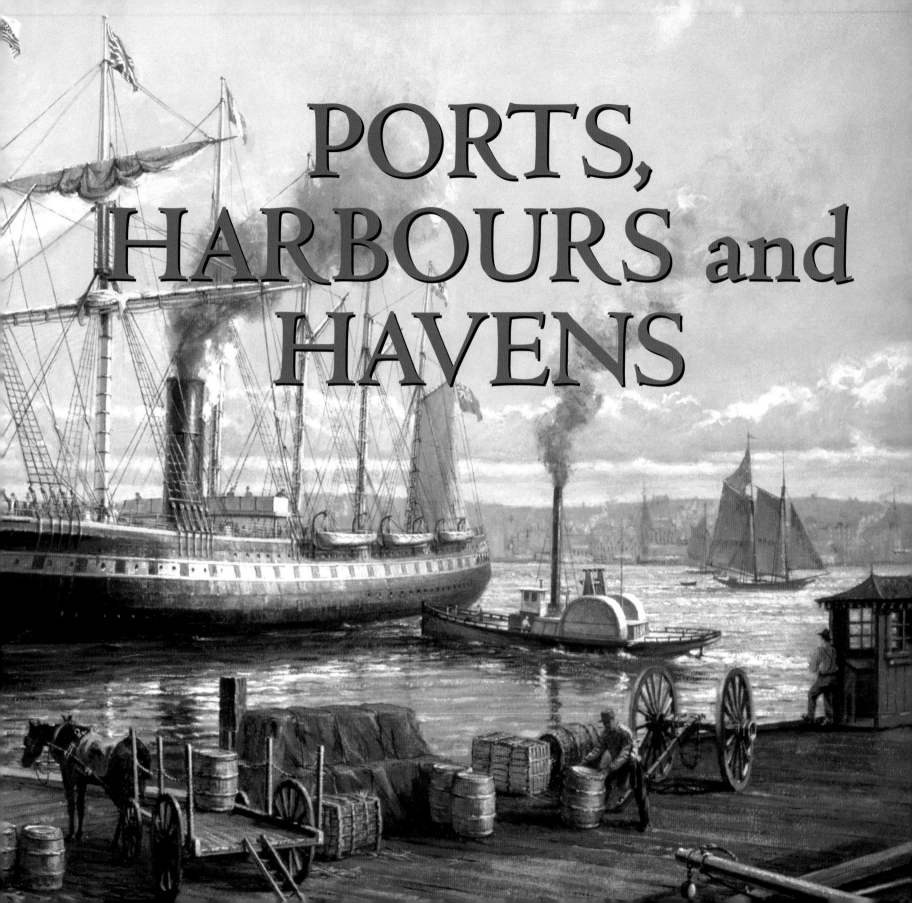

PORTS, HARBOURS and HAVENS

Previous page: **THE STEAM SHIP *GREAT BRITAIN*, AT SOUTH STREET AFTER HER MAIDEN VOYAGE TO NEW YORK IN 1845**

The SS *Great Britain*, designed by Brunel and built in 1843, now lies almost fully restored in the dock where she was constructed at Bristol. She was the first iron-hulled screw driven vessel designed for transoceanic passenger trade. She made her crossing to New York in fourteen days 21 hours. After four more crossings she began the Australian run in 1852 and continued to carry emigrants to a new life in the colonies and particularly to Victoria (where gold had been discovered) for a quarter of a century. The SS *Great Britain* saw war service in the Crimea, then resuming her Australia service by 1876 had completed 32 round trips! She went through several changes of engines and rig moving from a six-masted single funnel to become the world's largest three-masted sailing cargo vessel.

In 1886, after nearly being wrecked, she arrived in Port Stanley in the Falklands where she languished as a storage hulk until the 1960s. A group of enthusiasts proposed her salvage and transported her back to England and she was installed in the same dock in Bristol where she had been built. Now fully restored, she is a splendid ship to visit.

Commissioned by the SS *Great Britain* Trust, I chose to depict her on her maiden voyage arriving at South Street New York on August 10th 1845. My wife and I visited New York and traced the original landing place. We learned much from the South Street Museum and my wife advised me on American costumes of the era. Knowing the hour of arrival I checked the sun's angle and the reach of the shadows. Perhaps this was going too far?

THE SS *GREAT BRITAIN* ARRIVING AT LIVERPOOL

The SS *Great Britain* is depicted arriving at Liverpool from Australia in December 1861. The ship carried 691 persons including the All England Cricketing Eleven. She is flying her 'paying off' pennant and there is a Pilot Jack on the foremast indicating a Pilot on board. On the mizzen mast, the flags show the ship's number.

A NEWFOUNDLER DEPARTS FROM FECAMP, FRANCE c.1910

One of the staple foods of France at this time was salted cod. This was fished by such three-masted vessels as this which would sail across to Newfoundland where small dinghies or dories were sent out to fish on the Grand Banks. Fleets of such craft would go out for six months at a time and the cod would be laid down in salt to preserve it.

It is Sunday morning and the townsfolk, some coming from Mass, are gathering to chat or witness a familiar departure, familiar, because in their hey-day as many as seventy three departures took place in a year.

I researched this in Fecamp and can vouch for the fact that many of the buildings, the little bridge and the Chapelle de Notre Dame du Salut, still look the same today.

DRAWINGS

For the French patrons who commissioned the painting, I made three suggestions: Fecamp, Le Havre and Pornic.

The latter two are illustrated here.

THE TEA SHIP *FALCON* PASSING PORTSMOUTH

Launched in 1826, she was designed as a private yacht but with her full rig and general appearance she resembled a '20 gun ship of war'. For 10 years she proved a highly impressive flagship to the Royal Yacht Squadron.

In 1836 she was sold to Baring Brothers for use in the China Trade in which they came to consider her faster than any other vessel. After a refit in 1839, bought by Jardine Matheson, she operated out of Calcutta carrying opium to Macau until she disappears from records in the 1850s.

The painting was bought through Christie's and I met the new owner, who had travelled from Aachen, Germany. He had been a marine architect and had designed the cowl which you sometimes see surrounding the propellers of large ships such as liners and tankers. It was a very rewarding meeting.

This painting now hangs in the permanent collection of the recently opened large International Maritime Museum Hamburg, Germany.

DUNKERQUE HARBOUR, FRANCE 1909

The barque being towed out towards the sea is one of Antoine Borde's fleet which sailed to Chile to collect nitrate to fertilize the fields of Flanders. At that time, Dunkerque was not only an important commercial port but also a naval base, home to some sixteen torpedo boats and engaged in the development of mini submarines.

The Second World War saw Dunkerque much damaged and it is very different today. The painting was exhibited there in 1987. It attracted the interest of a number of the town's elders and I wondered how the painting compared with their pre-war memories. There must have been general approval because Senator–Mayor purchased it for the town's Musée des Beaux Arts.

DUNKERQUE HARBOUR, THE MINI SUBMARINE

My Dunkerque Harbour picture was illustrated in the American magazine *Sea History*. In the text I mentioned that the port was used for the development of mini-submarines one of which, the *Phoque* was seen on the left of the picture. This was seriously questioned by some of the magazine's readers. The editor wrote telling me this and asked for a reply. I was able to send photographs and a history of facts to show that indeed France, in 1909, was one of the pioneers in this field.

CIRCULAR QUAY, SYDNEY

Sydney Cove was the site of the initial landing of the First Fleet in Port Jackson. Circular Quay was originally used for shipping and became a very busy port. Hundreds of large square rigged ships would trade from Circular Quay to Europe during the latter part of the nineteenth century, particularly in the wool trade. From 1885 to 1894, the *Cutty Sark* carried some 46,000 bales – weighing a grand total of 18.6 million pounds to ports in England and Belgium. Sometimes as many as nine clippers would set out from Sydney and race towards the English Channel where records of their sailing times would be kept. Such a race started in 1885 between October 5th and 24th. The *Cutty Sark* and *Thermopylae* were great rivals and on this occasion, in spite of bad weather and delays, the *Cutty Sark* made the passage in 73 days against the *Thermopylae's* 80. The rest of the wool fleet straggled in over the next three weeks.

THE *QUEVILLY* IN DIEPPE, FRANCE ARRIVING FROM THE USA AROUND 1905

The *Quevilly* was the late nineteenth century equivalent of the modern giant oil tanker. A steel-hulled four master, she carried some 3,400 tonnes of crude oil in barrels from Philadelphia to an important oil refinery at Dieppe. Much of the rest of the picture is still recognisable in Dieppe today.

MOONLIGHT DUNKERQUE

A heavily loaded barque is being slowly towed into the harbour. She belongs to Antoine Borde's fleet which had recently moved its main operation from Nantes to the booming Channel port of Dunkerque.

HMS *TRINCOMALEE* VISITING HARTLEPOOL 1862

Trincomalee is making a courtesy visit for recruitment, showing a Pilot Jack at the bowsprit and sailors trimming the sails to perfection. The oldest Royal Navy vessel afloat, she was built in 1817 in India. The Napoleonic wars had used up so many trees in ships' construction that she was contracted out to an Indian shipyard. Fortunately, she was built from teak and therefore weathered much better than HMS *Victory* for example, in which there now only remains approximately 10% of the original timber.

HMS *Trincomalee* has been wonderfully restored at West Hartlepool and represents a fine example of an eighteenth century Royal Naval frigate used for a wide variety of roles in the first part of the nineteenth century. The painting was created in cooperation with the Trincomalee Trust using plans of the ship and I constructed a model of the port from 1860 maps to establish what would have been seen from Jackson's Dock.

BROOKLYN BRIDGE AND THE EAST RIVER, NEW YEAR
c.1883

In mid-stream, a tug is easing out a full-rigged ship to start its voyage. Just to the right is one of the Starin Line excursion boats which did such good business on the river. Nearby are Piers 28 and 29. To the left, the nearest ship looks as if she is getting ready to be assisted by the tug alongside to get underway. Hoping to still receive some passengers, she advertises her passage to San Francisco on a sheet attached to the foremast – a lengthy voyage around Cape Horn.

The barque to the right is still unloading long timbers from her special bow ports and bales from below decks using the donkey engine on the pier and one of her own spars as a crane. Also on the pier we can see a barrel repairer's hut and a merchant measuring a length of chain.

No doubt the great attraction to any visitor to this part of the East River, would be the splendid recently opened Brooklyn Bridge.

THE *BRIDGETOWN* AND OTHER CRAFT HOVE-TO OFF THE SEVEN SISTERS

The wind having fallen away completely, the *Bridgetown* and other craft lie becalmed and hove-to close to the Seven Sisters chalk cliffs in Sussex, England. Whilst waiting for a fresh breeze, they exchange news and views.

THE TUG *TIPPER* TOWING THE *BRIDGETOWN*

In almost windless conditions, the *Tipper* tows the *Bridgetown* across Seaford Bay near Newhaven. The *Bridgetown* was built in 1857 by John Gray whose yard lay on the west bank of the River Ouse very close to Newhaven town centre. It surprises us now to think how such small yards could regularly build oceangoing merchantmen. The *Bridgetown* had a length of 132 feet and a tonnage of 358. She had a good working life of 25 years eventually foundering on a beach at Durban, South Africa, in July 1882.

THE *PASSAT* AT HAMBURG

In 1872, the world's sailing fleet was greater than it had ever been; by 1945 it had virtually disappeared. Many of the great square riggers had been sunk and of course steam ships were everywhere. A major exception to this trend was Gustav Erikson, a Finnish ship owner who operated out of Marienhamn in the Aland Islands. During the 1920s and '30s, he built up and successfully operated the world's last sailing fleet of four masted sailing ships which were rigged so that they needed only small crews. The *Passat* carried nitrate from Chile to Europe and grain to Europe from Australia. She made her last Cape Horn voyage in 1949 and is now maintained afloat at Travemunde.

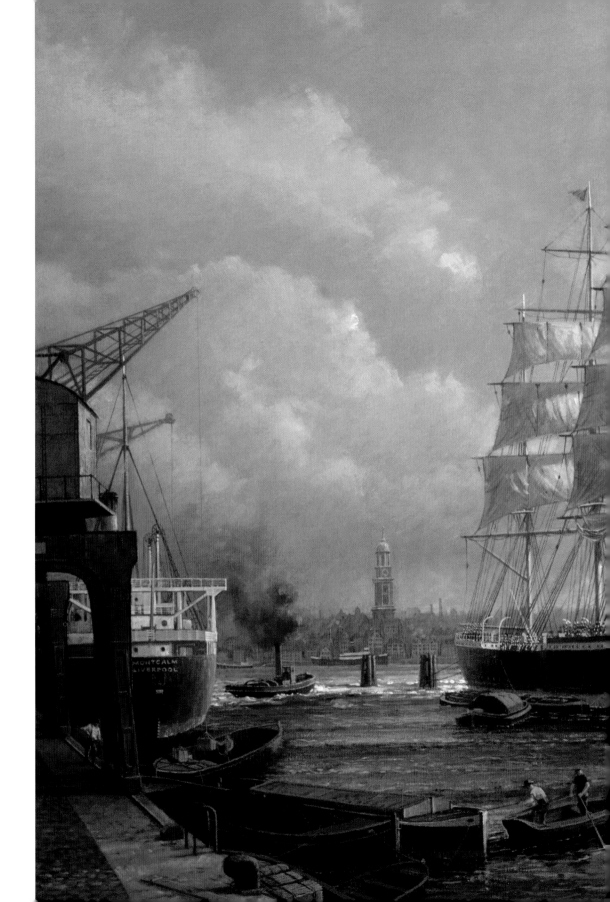

COLLIER ON BRIGHTON BEACH

Many colliers were almost flat bottomed to allow them to run up on a beach at high tide. They stayed there during low tide for horse drawn carts to unload them and enable coal men to deliver coal to the townsfolk.

BRIGHTON FORESHORE BETWEEN WEST STREET AND THE WEST PIER – 1885

Though not a port, Brighton was busy with craft along the shore and going to and from the pier. In the painting the conditions are so calm that the brig in the foreground is swinging slowly on her mooring and she is able to set almost all her sails to dry. Behind her, a fishing vessel, catching the morning light in her sails, is ghosting slowly by. At the beach, a flat bottomed collier is being unloaded at the foot of West Street. Nearby are some men's bathing machines – mixed bathing not being sanctioned in Brighton until 1889. Mid picture was the site of a thriving fish market near East Street. The Chain Pier was a great asset to the town, visited by Queen Victoria, served by paddle steamers and painted by both Constable and Turner. The pier survived until 1896 when it was destroyed by a storm.

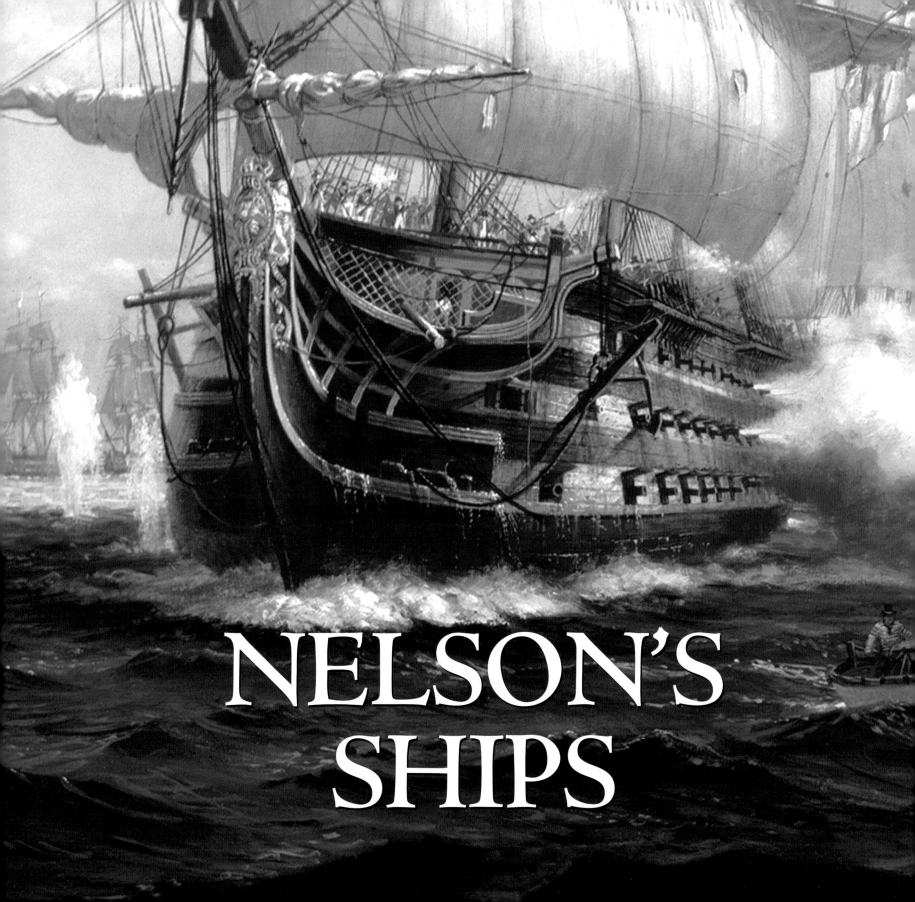

NELSON'S SHIPS

BATTLE OF THE NILE, AUGUST 1st 1798

Having searched the Mediterranean, Nelson finally found the enemy in Egypt. The French, moored in a line in the bay of Aboukir, thought that Nelson would not approach until the next day and then only on their starboard side. Instead, the battle began at sunset and the British attacked on both sides of the French line. Here Nelson's *Vanguard* is engaging *Le Spartiate* (centre) with *Theseus* attacking from the shore side. The battle went on through the night. When morning broke, it was upon devastation. "Victory is not a name strong enough for such a scene" said Nelson. Of the fourteen French ships, all but four were destroyed or captured. The enemy had experienced a large scale reverse and Napoleon's Expedition had been compromised.

LA SERIEUSE
Fr

THESEUS

LE SPATIATE (Fr)

LE CONQUERANT
(Fr)

VANGUARD
Nelson

BATTLE OF THE NILE, THE FIRST SKETCH

This was the sketch for my first painting of the battle. Nelson's *Vanguard* is to the right. When I had nearly completed the painting I was advised that probably Nelson would have been nearer the French line. Reluctantly, I created a new work which eventually turned out to be well received. From a painter's point of view I preferred the first painting which, fortunately, was sold quite quickly.

THE BATTLE OF COPENHAGEN APRIL 2nd 1801

With Nelson as second in command to Admiral Sir Hyde Parker, a fleet was sent to the Baltic early in 1801 following Denmark's decision to join the "Armed Neutrality" against British interests. Hyde Parker's orders were to capture or destroy the Danish fleet lying off Copenhagen.

At the beginning, the Danes being in a strong position, British losses mounted alarmingly so Hyde Parker signalled HMS *Elephant*, Nelson's flagship, to discontinue the engagement. Nelson, disagreeing with this strategy, then made his famous gesture. Placing his telescope to his blind eye to look at the signal he turned to his flag Captain and said "I really do not see the signal." The battle therefore continued and after prolonged fighting a cease fire was agreed with the British as victors.

Nelson already had his ideas about strategy before the battle and had discussed these with his Captains whom he called his "Band of brothers". Completely loyal to him, they supported his decision to continue to fight. Such loyalty was further exemplified at the Nile and Trafalgar.

96

HMS *VICTORY* LEADING THE LINE AT THE BATTLE OF TRAFALGAR

Nelson's *Victory* is seen leading the fleet off Cape Trafalgar at 11.30 am October 21st 1805 some thirty minutes before the start of the battle. Collingwood leads the second column in the *Royal Sovereign*. *Victory* is flying Nelson's favourite and final signal "Engage the enemy more closely".

The painting was commissioned by the Mott MacDonald Group Ltd to mark their merger with Ewebank Preece Ltd at their fine new premises in Brighton.

VICTORY RAKES *BUCENTAURE* AS SHE BREAKS THROUGH THE FRENCH AND SPANISH LINE

At approximately 1 pm, *Victory* broke through the line under the stern of *Bucentaure* and ahead of *Redoutable*. The *Victory's* double-shotted guns fired into the French flagship delivering a blow from which she could not recover.

This large painting 5'x 2'10" was commissioned by Mott MacDonald as a gift to its Chairman upon his retirement from the company. I was most pleased that Mr Beresford thereby got a leaving present which recollected his recent role in the company and reflected his great interest in Nelson's achievements in the Napoleonic wars.

THE BATTLE OF TRAFALGAR – THE DECISIVE ACTION

In the summer of 1805 Napoleon planned an invasion of England and assembled a large fleet of thirty three French and Spanish battleships at Cadiz. Nelson was sent to command the British fleet blockading Cadiz and to attack the enemy force. Thus on October 21st 1805 there began the most decisive sea battle ever fought. Of the thirty three ships, eighteen were taken, four escaped only to be caught later and the remainder struggled back to Cadiz .Effectively the allied enemy force had ceased to exist. The ferocious battle caused a great number of casualties. Among these was Nelson himself, struck by a musket ball. He was carried below and died some three hours later, but with knowledge that the battle had been won. His last words were "Thank God I have done my duty".

HMS *VICTORY* BEING TOWED UP TO GIBRALTAR BY *NEPTUNE* AFTER THE BATTLE OF TRAFALGAR

Nelson's flagship had borne the brunt of the fighting and, tragically, had lost her commander. Thus she was one of the British ships most in danger from the storm which followed the battle. It was immediately obvious to her loyal crew and those in the ships around her that HMS *Victory* had to be saved at all cost. Therefore, at 11 am on October 24th she was taken in tow by *Polyphemus* but the heavy seas caused her to become uncontrollable. She was let go and drifted until on October 27th she was retaken by *Neptune* and towed into Gibraltar the following day. There she was quickly made seaworthy with temporary repairs and began her slow journey carrying Nelson's body home to England.

**THR SCHOONER *PICKLE* OFF FALMOUTH BRINGING NEWS OF THE VICTORY AT TRAFALGAR
AND THE DEATH OF NELSON, NOVEMBER 1805**

Whilst Nelson's death and the great victory took place on October 21st 1805 it was to be two weeks before England received the extraordinary news. Vice Admiral Collingwood selected the schooner *Pickle* to carry the Trafalgar despatches to England. It took six days, however, to collect reports from the scattered fleet, only then could Lieutenant J. R. Lapenotiere on October 26th sail the *Pickle* the thousand miles from Cape Trafalgar to Falmouth. From there, with the aid of twelve changes of horses, the despatches were delivered to the Admiralty at 1 am on November 5th.

106

HMS FOUDROYANT TAKEN UNDER TOW TO VISIT COASTAL RESORTS IN 1896

The 80 gun *Foudroyant* was Nelson's flagship from **1780 to 1799** when she served in the Napoleonic War and in South America. Refitted in 1815 she served as a guard ship at Plymouth and then as a gunnery training ship. In 1890 she was sold to the philanthropist Mr Wheatly Cobb who restored her to become a sail training ship for youngsters who sought a career in the Royal Navy.

The ship is shown being taken under tow to coastal resorts to raise funds and recruit trainees. Unfortunately, she was driven on shore in a gale and foundered on Blackpool sands 16 June 1897.

Smitheman

HMS *VICTORY* BEING TOWED INTO NO 2 DOCK IN 1922

The HMS *Victory* ended her operational career in 1812 but continued to serve as a flagship moored at Portsmouth Harbour. Restored in No 2 Dry Dock – now to her appearance as at Trafalgar – she is still an H.M. Ship in commission, the oldest serving warship of any navy. This, of course, was the end of her life at sea but she would not exist if it had not been decided to restore her. One of the devoted enthusiasts for her restoration was that fine artist William Wyllie who spent much time aboard *Victory*.

It was a small etching by Wyllie which gave me the idea for this painting.

HMS *VICTORY*, HOVE-TO OFF PORTSMOUTH, FIRING A SALUTE TO VALIANT SAILORS

Victory was greatly damaged in the battle and had to be towed home to be restored. She continued to serve but underwent several refits over the years until, in 1922, she entered No 2 Dock in Portsmouth to be preserved. In recent times she has been restored to her original appearance as at Trafalgar, continuing to fly the White Ensign as an Admiral's flagship for the Second Sea Lord/Commander in Chief, Naval Home Command.

Here we see *Victory* in the evening, entirely at peace, paying homage to all those who had gallantly served at sea.

CROWN AGENTS STAMPS OF HMS *VICTORY*

For the anniversary of the Battle of Trafalgar in 2005, the Crown Agents, who are responsible for producing stamps for eleven countries (seven of them UK overseas territories), wanted their stamps to celebrate the anniversary.

They chose to reproduce a close-up from my painting of *"Victory* leading the line" on stamps for each of these countries. The unique aspect of these stamps was wherever wood was represented, for example, on the hull and spars, tiny fibres of wood from HMS *Victory* were incorporated in the printing. These could just be seen and easily felt … Ironically, the printing expertise was French!

ADVENTURES

THE AMERICAN CLIPPER *ELECTRIC*

The *Electric* is seen passing the bay of Guanabarra, Rio de Janeiro, with the Sugarloaf Mountain off her starboard bow in1854. She was built in 1853, launched on September 5th and first operated in the transatlantic trade between New York and Le Havre. The painting illustrates her only passage between New York and San Francisco which she made in 109 days. Upon her return, she resumed her role on the transatlantic route. In the 1860s she was sold to a Hamburg company and going under the North German flag still as *Electric*, she ran as a packet between Hamburg and New York. On November 7th 1872, in latitude 40 degrees north, longitude 50 degrees west she was abandoned leaking and nearly full of water. Her crew were picked up by the *Helmesbrand* and landed at Queenstown.

THE EAST INDIAMAN *GOTHEBORG* IN THE PEARL RIVER,
CHINA, JULY 1744

Founded in 1731 the Swedish East India Company was an important influence on the economic life of Sweden, especially in its trade with China. The *Gotheborg* is being loaded with bales of rattan from a barge. At left is a busy settlement, at right an old European hulk now acting as a repair depot for visiting ships. Tragically, the *Gotheborg* ran aground and sank on her return home in September 1745. Fortunately, much of her huge cargo was salvaged.

Recently, the ship has been constructed anew, using many of the original building techniques and has repeated her original journey, this time arriving home safely.

MOBY DICK

Many people know of the tale of Captain Ahab's pursuit of the whale Moby Dick from the novel by Herman Melville. Few know that it was based on a true event when the whaler *Essex* was sunk by an enraged sperm whale far out in the Pacific in November 1820, an event which set in train one of the most dramatic sea stories of all time.

A central character in the story was Owen Chase, a young ambitious man who at 22 was First Mate of the *Essex*. Owen lived and suffered through the whole ordeal and became the subject of a narrative from which Herman Melville drew inspiration for his novel.

The photograph is of a ship model in my possession which was once in the Newhaven Maritime Museum. The documentation states that it was carved by Owen Chase.

THE *ESSEX JUNIOR* A SOURCE FOR THE BOOK *MOBY DICK*

This model relates to the Nantucket Whaler which was rammed and sunk by a bull whale on November 20th 1820. A survivor, 'boat steerer' Owen Chase, was rescued from a whale boat after a horrendous journey of ninety days across the Pacific during which the survivors had resorted to a cannibalistic lottery. The ramming of the *Essex Junior* was the source for Herman Melville's book *Moby Dick*.

Owen Chase carved the hull of the model.

HMS *BOUNTY* AT OPAREE BAY

HMS *Bounty* had been in Matavai Bay since October 1783. Helped by the natives, the crew had been growing breadfruit plants to be taken to the West Indies. At Christmas, storms forced Captain Bligh to move anchorage to Oparee Bay. The painting shows the ship, now filled with over a thousand breadfruit plants, ready to depart amid "a vast excess of grief" and many exchanges of gifts. *Bounty* is hove-to with her main mast sails backed and ready to be towed out of the bay by two boats, one of which is near the bow with Fletcher Christian at the helm, the other still being lowered from the foremast main course spar. The Tahitian's chief Tynah's last words were "May God bless and protect you forever". He could not have envisioned that within three weeks, Captain Bligh and seventeen loyalists would be cast adrift and that two hundred years hence the story of the 'Mutiny on the Bounty' would still have so much potency.

THE *ST PAUL* GROUNDED AT CUCKMERE HAVEN BY A FRENCH PRIVATEER IN 1747

The *St Paul* left London in 1747 with a cargo including £20,000 sterling bound for Virginia USA via Portsmouth. Abreast of Cuckmere Haven, near Seaford, she was attacked by a French Privateer. The *St Paul* grounded and was boarded by the French who, it appeared, broke out the alcohol and quickly became drunk. Spotted by locals from along the coast, an attempt was made to recapture the *St Paul*. Others succeeded in dragging "His Majesty's cannon" from Seaford Head to a cliff overlooking the scene. This was threat enough to keep off the Privateer. Eventually the *St Paul* was refloated and was able to continue her voyage. Some 83 locals benefited from the £1000 salvage money distributed,

THE *FLYING CLOUD'S* BRUSH WITH THE *N.B. PALMER*
IN THE SOUTH ATLANTIC, JULY 1ST 1852

Of this great American Clipper, Longfellow wrote:

She starts — she moves — she seems to feel

The thrill of life along her keel

And spurning with her foot the ground

With one exciting joyous bound

She leaps into the ocean's arms

Though she was the largest merchantman yet built, she was a fast ship. The well documented incident in the painting concerned another famous clipper, the *N.B. Palmer*. Both ships were bound from New York to San Francisco. The *Cloud* left eight days ahead of its rival yet Captain Low on the *Palmer* managed to catch up at 32 degrees south. Challenged by the *Palmer's* performance, Captain Cressy crammed on all sail to the studding sails (extra square sails run out on extensions to the yards) and left the *Palmer* for good. In fact, at that time the *Flying Cloud* was the fastest clipper afloat, able to average 15 ½ knots over a 374 nautical mile run, at times exceeding 18 knots.

FROM THE LOG BOOK OF THE *FELICITY*,
WEST INDIAMAN OF TRURO

A half-cask containing the log-book from which these extracts are taken
was picked up by the barque *Emelia* on August 12th 1820.

"July 27: Yesterday met a large topsail schooner. He
asked if I could give him some water. A longboat
came alongside and seven men came on deck. Drew
pistols, bound me, took money and water. Took six of
my crew, leaving the rest bound.

August 6: Two crew sick, think Slavers brought small
pox on board.

August 9. Dismasted by sudden squall of hurricane
force – too few crew to reduce sail quick enough.
Lost two men overboard. Ship leaking badly.

August 11: Rest of hands left ship in jolly boat while
I was in hold trying to locate leak.

Ship sinking: One of sick died last night.
God help us."

THE S.S. *GREAT BRITAIN* ON ARRIVAL AT HOBSON'S BAY MELBOURNE ON HER FIRST AUSTRALIAN VOYAGE

Seven years after her launch, *Great Britain* changed owners and was greatly modified and improved by new engines, two funnels, four masts instead of six and a new long deckhouse built above the top deck. Arriving near Melbourne she would moor in Hobson's Bay (the River Yarra being too shallow at that time) and tenders would come out to take off the passengers.

The prison hulk at left was one of several created to cope with crime which had grown with the discovery of gold.

The painting was commissioned by the SS *Great Britain* Trust.

THE CUTTY SARK RACING THE *THERMOPYLAE*
IN THE SOUTH CHINA SEA, 1872

On her third voyage in 1872, the *Cutty Sark* got the long awaited chance to race the *Thermopylae* home in the same weather and under the same conditions. Both left the mouth of the Shanghai River on June 18th. Both were held up by fog. When the weather cleared, they sped down the China Sea, and exchanged the lead several times over the next 4 weeks. Eventually, the *Cutty Sark* gained a 400 mile lead …

THE *SPIRIT OF BIRMINGHAM* IN THE SOUTHERN OCEAN

Lisa Clayton in her yacht *Spirit of Birmingham* was the first woman to make a full circumnavigation around the world single handed, nonstop and unassisted.

I had the pleasure and privilege of working with her on this painting. I did three different studies and she chose a version which she felt represented the moment when sailing toward Cape Horn, she finally felt that she would reach home again.

She had lived through a terrible storm, had capsized seven times, on two occasions of which the boat went through 360 degrees. Lisa was thrown overboard but her safety line somehow snapped her back. She was knocked unconscious for nine hours and believed it was the end. After nine days the winds eased and she began to repair the damage and begin sailing again. The painting shows her full of hope pressing for home.

THE
PRESENT

A LONG WAY FROM HOME, *THE SPIRIT OF BIRMINGHAM* **IN THE SOUTHERN OCEAN**

A second version of Lisa Clayton's record breaking round the world voyage focusing less on the frightening sea but more on the sense of isolation felt by Miss Clayton.

KASKELOT OFF NEWHAVEN

Kaskelot is a replica of a nineteenth-century three-masted barque, one of the last proper square riggers to be built. She was built for the Danish Government in 1948 as a trading and supply ship for remote Greenland settlements. She also served as a hospital for the Eskimos and then a fisheries support vessel in the Faroes until the 1970s. Since 1981 she has done much film and TV work featuring in a number of fine films. She is also used extensively as a sail training vessel.

KASKELOT,
Alternative Design

BRIXHAM, A TRAWLER BY THE STEPS

A COASTAL STEAMER BEING TOWED INTO NEWHAVEN.

This was commissioned by Dr Colin Morris who for many years broadcast "Thought for Today" on the *Today* radio programme. He writes his broadcasts and books in an apartment overlooking this harbour.

THE *BELLE TOUT* COMING HOME

I was commissioned by the owner of a Devonshire crabber to paint his boat the *Belle Tout*. The attraction was that he would take me out on a typical day's work, mid-channel out of Newhaven. Twenty miles off the coast, we arrived at the buoys marking where he had laid out 120 pots, 48 hours previously. We were immediately challenged by a continental vessel which claimed fishing rights over this area of sea. Apparently there are no maps of rights – it is all done by gentleman's agreement. My ability to speak French to the skipper helped sort out the matter and we started hauling in the crab pots which were then emptied into barrels on deck.

I settled down on the deck at the prow drawing. From time to time, a wave would break over the boat and I and my sketch book were soaked but we managed to dry the sketch book on an exhaust pipe from the engine. I did a deck painting for my host but also this one which tries to give the feeling of the boat settling down into calm water after having been bounced about in a choppy English Channel for 11 hours.

THE PUNTA DELLA DOGANA AND SANTA MARIA DELLA SALUTE

CADAQUES, A PRETTY RESORT ON THE COSTA BRAVA, SPAIN

UFFA FOX BOATYARD

Uffa Fox was a brilliant fast small-boat designer. During the war he designed a lifeboat capable of being carried by an aircraft and released by a parachute over the target. The boat had sails, an engine and supplies. His invention saved many 'ditched' airmen's lives.

A family business, it is now run by Uffa's nephew and it is still producing innovative designs.

This was painted on a trip when we took students to the South Coast.

THE SAIL TRAINING VESSEL *SORLANDET*

Visiting Kristiansand, Norway, I was introduced to the Captain of the impressive white-hulled Sail Training Ship *Sorlandet* (Southlands). She was built by Blom and Voss at Hamburg and has taken part in many Tall Ships Races and events.

The Captain, himself a marine painter, invited me to stay aboard so I did some sketching and later painted this record of a night time coffee break.

A FRENCH SCHOONER LEAVING NEWHAVEN HARBOUR

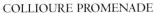

COLLIOURE PROMENADE

This is a simple scene from across the bay of Collioure. We have taken our summer holidays in this area for over thirty years. The light is just as remarkable as Matisse claimed when he wrote to Vlaminck in Paris saying that he should come down and work here.

Vlaminck did so – by bicycle – carrying his painting gear! It takes me ten hours hard driving. Vlaminck thought the light and colour justified his journey. I feel the same.

LA CAPTE

A seaside village close to Hyeres has a small population of some 600 inhabitants but its port offers more than 300 moorings during the season. It is ideal for small craft to explore the nearby islands of Porqueroles, Port-Cros and Le Levant. As a family we did this with great pleasure. This painting is very evocative of early morning in the little port.

COLLIOURE HARBOUR

In the early twentieth century, Collioure became a centre of artistic activity and a host to Fauvism. Derain, Braque, Matisse, Picasso and Mackintosh were all inspired by its castle, medieval streets, church and typical Mediterranean bay.

The novelist, Patrick O'Brien, writer on the Napoleonic naval wars lived in the town from 1949 until his death in 2000.

HMS *SHOREHAM*

HMS *Shoreham* is a Royal Navy Sandown class mine hunter which was commissioned in Shoreham by Sea on 20th July 2002. She has a crew of 35, weighs 500 tons and is 52.9 meters long. Four RN ships have previously been called *Shoreham*. The original was built in Shoreham in 1694.

The painting was commissioned by Mr and Mrs Borbone to celebrate the appointment of their son Nicholas as the new Commanding Officer of HMS *Shoreham* in 2007.

ALMIRANTE

Almirante was a banana boat working for Fyffes. It got into trouble in the Channel when its cargo shifted. The tug *Meeching* went out from Newhaven to tow it into port. I was friendly with the *Meeching's* Captain who phoned me and invited me to come along to see her towed in. It was a fascinating trip, so I painted it.

SAGRES II

One of a number of such sail training ships this handsome vessel was built in 1937 by Blom and Voss at Hamburg for the German Navy. Eventually, she was acquired by the Portuguese also for sail training and renamed *Sagres II*. She has taken part in the Tall Ships Races, always easily recognisable from the red Portuguese crosses on her square sails.

For imformation concerning commissions and prints please e-mail: **fsmitheman@btinternet.com**
For various lithographic and giclee prints, including signed and limited editions e-mail: **www.marineartists.co.uk** and **www.rnmuseumshop.co.uk**